A 21 DAY JOU

Embracing Mystery

Anna Maher

FOREWORD BY STEVE BACKLUND

Embracing Mystery © copyright 2015
Anna Maher
Catalyst Ministries
www.chuckandannamaher.com

Cover design and pagination: Renee Evans
Editing: Melissa Amato

All Scripture quotations, unless otherwise indicated, are taken from the Holy Bible, New International Version®, NIV®. Copyright ©1973, 1978, 1984, 2011 by Biblica, Inc.™ Used by permission of Zondervan. All rights reserved worldwide. www.zondervan.com The "NIV" and "New International Version" are trademarks registered in the United States Patent and Trademark Office by Biblica, Inc.™

To order copies of this book, please visit www.chuckandannamaher.com. Bulk rates are available upon request.

ISBN: 978-0-9861797-0-9

ACKNOWLEDGEMENTS

I want to say thank to a few of the people without which this devotional would not have been possible.

Mom, thanks for modeling a love for God's Word to me for as long as I can remember. Thanks for all the Bible studies you have written over the years. Your gift has brought many into deeper revelation of the Bible, as well as deeper relationship with God.

Dad, thank you for modeling to me the love of our heavenly Father so well. Without your love, encouragement, and affirmation, I would not be the person I am today. You are the best dad I know!

Steve and Wendy, thanks for believing in me before I believed in myself. Thank you for helping me develop my message, and teaching me about higher perspectives. You have been such a gift to Chuck and I.

Renee, thank you for making this book look good—I love what you have done. More than all the work you have done, I appreciate your friendship through the ups and downs of life. Thank you for both.

Melissa, thank you for your amazing editing skills. Your ability to give feedback in a positive, encouraging way astounds me. Thanks for all your hard work and encouragement.

Chuck, thank you for loving me on my best days and my grumpy days. Thank you for encouraging me to write and to be all that God has called me to be. Your kindness has taught me so much. I love you with all my heart!

ENDORSEMENTS

Anna's book *Embracing Mystery* is a book that will bring you into a closer walk with God. This book brings encouragement and it also challenges us to embrace God's mysteries. I believe that when we can trust God with our every day and fully believe Him, we will be able to embrace His mysteries. There is a peace that comes in surrender to His ways even when we don't understand those things in our lives that make no sense to us. God loves us and I believe this book *Embracing Mystery* will bring us into more understanding of His great plan for our lives.

BENI JOHNSON
SENIOR LEADERSHIP TEAM OF BETHEL CHURCH, REDDING, CA

Many times we don't know what God is doing or even intending. We can get scared or hurt when we fill in the blanks ourselves. Knowing that God is good and only has plans of victory for us is vital. Through her own personal journey, Anna Maher has found the God of Hope. In the pages of *Embracing Mystery*, the reader will draw new strength and powerful expectations for living the life God has set before him or her. I highly recommend this devotional for your personal study or small group.

DANNY SILK

FOUNDER OF LOVING ON PURPOSE, SENIOR LEADERSHIP TEAM OF JESUS CULTURE, SACRAMENTO, CA

You will love this straightforward journey into the Father's heart, filled with expectation and hope. We learn to embrace mystery as Anna lays out practical insights and asks provoking questions to guide us along the way. I thoroughly enjoyed this study of hope!

KELLEY FESTE

SENIOR LEADERSHIP TEAM OF KINGDOM LIFE CHURCH, SAN ANTONIO, TX

Anna Maher is a good friend and is someone I know to live what she believes on a daily basis. What Anna has put into the pages of *Embracing Mystery* is not just theory, but an honest and vulnerable look into the revelations the Lord has shown her through her own journey of learning to abide in hope, joy, and peace through all of life's unforeseen circumstances. This book serves as an informative guide through this journey while also leaving ample space for the reader to dialogue and receive from the Lord along the way. *Embracing Mystery* asks the types of questions that have the ability to adjust the way we view ourselves and our relationship with our Heavenly Father so that we can enjoy the fullness of life that the Lord has always intended for us. Happy reading.

JOAQUIN EVANS

DIRECTOR OF BETHEL ACTIVATION MINISTRIES,
BETHEL CHURCH, REDDING, CA

CONTENTS

FOREWORD
by Steve Backlund

I have known Anna Maher for many years. She is a spiritual daughter to my wife Wendy and me. Anna interned for me and she and her husband, Chuck, are important parts of our current ministry. (I frequently recommend them as guest speakers to ministries around the world.) Anna is a woman of wisdom, love, courage, and revelation. Every time I hear her speak, I receive much from the Lord, Because of this, I am thrilled that others get the opportunity to experience Anna through this book.

Embracing Mystery is a powerful tool to grow in intimacy with God, increase hope for the future, and strengthen beliefs in God's goodness. It will immerse you in Scripture, plus it has questions each day to connect your heart to God's heart. As a matter of fact, the questions she has each are worth the book alone. I believe the Holy Spirit will use them for you to hear from the Lord in a very special way.

Get ready to grow. Get ready for three weeks of renewing your mind. Get ready to embrace mystery like never before. Get ready for transformation. And get ready to enter into a new, hope-filled season of your life. Thanks, Anna, for breaking off a piece of your life and sharing it with us. We will never be the same again.

STEVE BACKLUND

INTRODUCTION

This book is designed to be an interactive journey between you and the Father. You will soon notice that *Embracing Mystery* is not written in a typical format. I believe that hope is a crucial part of our Christian faith, and that the principles of Scripture can be applied to our lives and any circumstances, and bear much fruit. In Romans 15:13, God calls Himself the God of all hope, and this devotional is a tool to go deeper in the revelation of who He is. I can't wait for you to begin this journey. Enjoy!

EMBRACING MYSTERY

The difference between embracing mystery and fearing
the unknown is all wrapped up in our perspective of
our Heavenly Father.
ANNA MAHER

Late one night I lay in my bed thinking about the future. I felt my mind start to drift into a place of worry. As I tossed different scenarios around, suddenly a voice cut through the darkness. I felt the Lord tell me, "Anna, your ability to embrace mystery or fear the unknown is all wrapped up in your perspective of Me as a Father."

I began to ponder His statement over the coming days and weeks. I made a decision that it was time to position myself in a place of embracing the mystery rather than letting fear grip my thoughts of the days to come. I want to invite you to join Me on this journey. I pray that we may be like Sarah, who did not give way to fear (1 Peter 3:6). More than that, I pray that an incredible excitement will overcome us when we think of the future. I pray that the strongholds of fear will be broken as we discover how good our heavenly Father is.

Welcome to the journey of embracing mystery!

Look up the word "mystery." What does it mean?

One of my favorite definitions is from Webster's 1828 dictionary. It says, "That which is beyond human comprehension until explained. In this sense, mystery often conveys the idea of something awfully sublime or important; something that excites wonder."

READ ISAIAH 60:1-5.

Look at verse 5. What does it mean to you "to look and be radiant"?

What about for your "heart to throb and swell with joy"?

Do you have an emotional reaction when you think about the future? If so, what is it?

Is it easy for you to believe that your heavenly Father wants you to have a happy emotional response to the things to come?

I've often read the beginning of Isaiah 60, but I am particularly struck with the fact that God wants my heart to throb and swell with delight. This thought kind of reminds me of a giddy junior high girl. Sometime after that is when this excitement about the future seems to fade away for a lot of us. We grow up. We move on. We become "realistic." The problem is I am not sure that was ever supposed to be our role.

About a year ago, we surprised my mother and sister-in-law with a trip to San Francisco. They are from the East Coast of Canada so they had never been there before. My husband's mother began dancing around our living room singing, "I am going to San Francisco." We laughed and loved her excitement. It's so fun to be able to bless someone who is visibly overjoyed by what you are giving!

I believe the Father's heart is for us to have an emotional response to the future. I think it brings joy to His heart when we trust Him to the point of being okay with the things we don't know. I believe it gives Him space to radically bless us.

What are some areas of mystery that you are facing now?

What would it look like for this area to exceed your expectations?

READ EPHESIANS 3:16-21.

Ask the Lord to grant you the power to grasp how wide and long and high and deep His love is for you.

Why do you think it mentions in verse 19 "love that surpasses knowledge"?

I think it's important to guard our hearts against exalting knowledge above Jesus Christ. Knowledge is a wonderful and important part of how we've been created, but we must caution ourselves from limiting the power of Almighty God to the facts we see. Jesus Christ is Truth, (John 14:6) and Truth is greater than facts. Love surpasses knowledge (Ephesians 3:19).

Do you believe He is able to do immeasurably more than all we ask or imagine? Why or why not?

I am excited for you–this is an incredible journey we are on! Let's pray a simple prayer to conclude today's lesson.

Father, I thank You that You have good things in store for me. I lay down my own understanding. I place my trust in You. I want to know You. Reveal Yourself to me. Show me the truth about who You are and how You see me. Amen.

THE FATHER

How deep the Father's love for us,
How vast beyond all measure
That He should give His only Son
To make a wretch His treasure.

How great the pain of searing loss,
The Father turns His face away
As wounds which mar the chosen One,
Bring many sons to glory.

Behold the Man upon a cross,
My sin upon His shoulders
Ashamed I hear my mocking voice,
Call out among the scoffers.

It was my sin that held Him there
Until it was accomplished
His dying breath has brought me life
I know that it is finished.

I will not boast in anything
No gifts, no power, no wisdom
But I will boast in Jesus Christ
His death and resurrection.

Why should I gain from His reward?
I cannot give an answer
But this I know with all my heart
His wounds have paid my ransom.

STUART TOWNEND

The key to embracing mystery is in the revelation of our heavenly Father. One obstacle can be our earthly father and our relationship (or lack thereof) with him. No matter what kind of father you have experienced here on earth, we must continually walk in the realization that our heavenly Father offers us something that our earthly father never could–perfection (Matthew 5:48).

I have an incredible dad who loves me fiercely. If I could choose a dad from all the men I have met, I would choose him. I am very, very thankful. He is extremely protective. When my now husband let him know his intentions toward me, my dad required a typed, one page essay on his biblical view of marriage AND a list of ten reasons why he wanted to marry me... Yes, I am from the south.

My dad is also a VERY hard worker. He is a tree farmer with calloused hands. He is the kind of man who works so hard that anytime he sits down, he is soon snoring. This is an incredibly admirable trait, for which I am thankful. Since children often take after their parents, this is also a trait that means I have to caution myself from working for things that have already been purchased for me. Grace is not by works lest any man (or woman) should boast (Ephesians 2:8).

I share that for the sake of vulnerability, and to open up our hearts to allow God to reveal Himself to us afresh and anew.

I know many of you have endured very tragic relationships with your father, and for that I am deeply sorry. I do feel a tremendous hope that for all of us there is a greater revelation of the heavenly Father's love coming our way no matter what our history may be!

What are some ways that your earthly father has modeled the heavenly Father to you? (Even if he is not a believer, try to find at least one way.)

READ LUKE 11:1-13.

What stands out to you from verses 2-4?

What do you think the Lord wants to show you through that?

READ VERSES 9-10 AGAIN.

Take some time to ask the Lord for a few things and list them out.

Do you find it easy to ask the Father for things? Why or why not?

He longs to give you good gifts. These gifts aren't based on your performance. His gifts are based on His goodness, not your works. He values you and created you in His image. Your value isn't based on what you've done or haven't done. Your value is based on the truth that He formed you in your mother's womb. You are not an accident. His hands intentionally fashioned you to become like Him.

Ask the Lord if there is anything hindering you from receiving good gifts from Him. If so, what is it?

Read the song at the beginning of this chapter and ask the Lord to reveal His love afresh and anew.

READ ROMANS 8:32.

How do we know that God loves us?

Sometimes we can look for something to prove that He loves us. We think if He does _____, then I'll know that He loves me. His love is already proven. It was proven 2,000 years ago on that cross. What I am not saying is that when you get the next thing you long for, that verifies that God loves you. God loves you. Period.

What I am saying is that because we KNOW that He loves us, we can trust Him. We can trust Him with our heart's desires. We can trust Him with the things we think He can't see about us. We can trust Him with the stuff we can't see. We can trust Him with the unknown in our lives.

I sense that there are things that the Father wants to speak directly to your heart. Will you quiet your heart before Him and ask Him how He sees you? Journal what you hear, feel, or sense here. Don't overthink this, just listen and write the words that come.

Take some time to process with the Father. Allow His love for you to penetrate to the deepest places within you.

Father, we receive Your love. You are perfect love.
Encounter us with Your love afresh and anew today.
Amen.

HE WITHHOLDS NO GOOD THING

God never withholds from His child that which His love and wisdom call good. God's refusals are always merciful—"severe mercies" at times, but mercies all the same. God never denies us our heart's desire except to give us something better.

ELISABETH ELLIOT

I love this Elisabeth Elliot quote. There was a season in my life when I sensed the Lord saying, "I am not withholding from you, I am protecting you." Things had not worked out the way I thought they should, and I was processing deep disappointment. In the midst of this, God was reminding me that He had the big picture in mind. He, like my dad, is fiercely protective of His girls. Like Elisabeth says, "God never denies us our hearts desire except to give us something better."

READ PSALM 84:11.

What do you think the Psalmist meant when he said God is a "sun and a shield"?

What does that mean to you personally?

The Psalm says, "He bestows favor." Have you ever tried to earn favor on your own? If so, how did that go?

Look up the word "favor," and write it's definition here:

Favor:

Have you ever felt that the Lord is "withholding" something from you? If so, what was it?

Unless there is something better He is going to give, He cannot withhold good from His children. It is against God's nature. God is love. One definition of love is choosing the highest good. Love always protects (1 Corinthians 13:7), but never withholds good things (Psalm 84:11).

Two-year-old boys love cars. Yet, I have never seen even the best of dads hand their two-year-old the keys to the family minivan. Does that mean they will never drive? No–it means that a good father knows his child, and at the appropriate time he will teach his son to drive. At the appropriate time, he will hand over the keys and allow that rite of passage. We can often be like the two-year-old, and if we don't immediately get handed the keys, we draw conclusions such as "WE WILL NEVER GET TO DRIVE!"

Just because you haven't received your promise yet does NOT mean you will never get it. It means that there is perhaps something better than you could imagine coming your way. Take heart—He is a good Father who loves to give good gifts!

Can you think of any times when you thought God was withholding something, but now you can see He was protecting you? If so, what happened?

READ PROVERBS 3:5-6.

What do you think it means to "lean not on your own understanding"?

My pastor often says, "We have to give up our right to understand." I've already touched on how our culture is very focused on knowledge. There is a saying that "knowledge is power." I am not saying that's not true, but we have to be careful. Are we giving all of our power (thoughts, energy, and attention) to what we know?

What does it say before "to lean not on your own understanding"?

What does that look like for you?

Ask the Holy Spirit if there are any areas where you may not be trusting God with all your heart? Write your response here:

Reflecting on what we've learned so far about our heavenly Father, take some time to surrender any areas you've struggled to give over to Him. This is not a time for condemnation; it's a time for freedom! Ultimately we are happiest when we are in a place of fully trusting Him.

THE POWER OF THE TONGUE

You can change your world by changing your words... Remember, death and life are in the power of the tongue.
JOEL OSTEEN

For the rest of this study, we will end each day with declarations. I believe that speaking the truth over our lives is a big key to seeing things change. Today I want to share with you the scriptural foundation for this concept.

READ JAMES 3:1-6.

What are some of the things that James compares with the tongue?

What do you think James is trying to communicate?

We can easily underestimate the power of the things we say. I am not saying this to instill fear in you, but my heart is to communicate how powerful the things we speak are. This offers us hope and a way to partner with God to see things shift in our lives!

What does Proverbs 18:21 say?

More than likely you have heard these scriptures before, and today I want to come at it from the positive side rather than the negative side. There is so much power in what we say, and we have the opportunity to speak life with our words!

What does Proverbs 12:14 say?

THE POWER OF THE TONGUE

READ EZEKIEL 37:1-10.

What did the Lord command Ezekiel to SAY to the dry bones?

What happened when Ezekiel prophesied to the dry bones?

It is important to notice that he didn't tell Ezekiel to DO something, He told Ezekiel to SAY something. He didn't ask Ezekiel to tell Him what he currently saw, He told Ezekiel to declare a better word over the dry bones!

We can often feel like we are being dishonest when we choose to focus on solutions rather than the problem at hand. We can ask for heaven's perspective and declare the Word over our current trials. This is a concept we find in the Bible. Jesus told us that with faith as small as a mustard seed, we can see great things move (Matthew 17:20).

What do we know about our God from Romans 4:17?

What did Jesus say in Matthew 19:26?

At one point, I was feeling hopeless about a particular area in my life. Proverbs 13:12 says, "Hope deferred makes the heart sick, but desire fulfilled is a tree of life"(NASB). I had experienced hope deferred a number of times in this area, and I was over it! As I drove to work in the mornings, I began to declare out loud, "Trees of life and no more heart sickness."

Within a matter of months, I had total breakthrough in this area! Our words are powerful.

Why do I think declarations are important? Romans 10:17 says that faith comes by hearing. When we speak truth over our lives, faith is imparted. I believe that it's often more about us hearing and believing than trying to convince God. It's about us aligning our hearts with the truth about who He is. The more we speak truth over our lives, the more we begin to believe the truth!

What did Jesus say in Matthew 17:20?

That should be encouraging for us! With faith as small as a mustard seed, we have the power to move mountains. Declarations are a tool that helps us align our hearts to heaven and operate in the authority that Jesus gave us here on earth.

I believe that our declarations should line up with the scriptures. As you work your way through this study, you will see, at the end of each day, how I rephrase scriptures for you to speak over your life. For today's lesson, I've included the scripture references.

I invite you to seek out the scriptures and create your own declarations to begin speaking over your life. I am excited for the breakthroughs to come!

Let's get started! Speak these truths over your life right now:

DECLARATIONS:

I am like a tree planted by the water; whatever I do prospers (Psalm 1:3).

My best days are ahead of me (2 Corinthians 3:18).

I can get excited about what the future holds (Proverbs 31:25).

No good thing is being withheld from my life (Psalm 84:11).

My Father loves to give me good gifts (Matthew 7:11).

I have more than enough (Psalm 34:9 and John 10:10).

PEACE

Peace is not the absence of trouble but the presence of Christ.
SHEILA WALSH

Who doesn't love peace? We may not talk about it very often, but even newborn babies are aware of its presence or absence. I used to work at a maternity home...a place for young girls with unplanned pregnancies. Occasionally, these girls and their newborn babies would live with me in a temporary situation. The young mother was struggling with the weight of caring for an infant. I would often come home from work to a crying baby. Within seconds of me holding the newborn, she would calm down and stop crying. My other roommate would marvel as she watched. The baby recognized peace and safety from infancy.

Peace isn't about perfect circumstances, soft music, and wonderfully scented candles. (Although all those things are so nice!) Peace is about what/who is holding you.

What are the names for Jesus in Isaiah 9:6?

READ ISAIAH 26:3.

How do we stay in perfect peace?

READ ISAIAH 26:12.

Who establishes peace?

PEACE

The Prince of Peace has come. He establishes peace for us. Our role is to keep our eyes on Him. When our attention is directed in the right place, peace re-enters our hearts and minds. Peace is always available; sometimes it's just neglected.

READ JOHN 16:17-33.

What is Jesus telling His disciples in this passage?

Why did He tell them to "take heart"?

The Greek word *tharseō* for "take heart" can also be translated, "be of good cheer, take courage." We don't have bravery and courage as a result of our own ability, but because He has overcome the world! They are not based on our own strength, but fully on His. That is good news!

READ PHILIPPIANS 4:4-7.

Paul kindly gives us what I like to call a four-step process to peace that passes all understanding.

What are these four steps?

1.

2.

3.

4.

Is there any area in your life where you are feeling a lack of peace? If so, where?

Again, we are not processing these areas to lead us to condemnation. We are here for freedom! We are on a journey to make a transfer from fearing the unknown to embracing mystery.

Those who look to Him are radiant,
their faces are never covered with shame.

PSALM 34:7

The goal here is always to look to Him. I want to invite you to take any area that's lacking peace through the four-step process so that you can possess the peace that passes all understanding.

DECLARATIONS:

I have the Prince of Peace living inside of me.

I possess a peace that passes all understanding.

I lean not on my own understanding.

Father, I thank You that You have made peace accessible to us no matter where we are. Thank You that greater are You within me, than he who is in the world. I thank You for flooding our homes with Your peace right now. Jesus, we thank You for coming to this world and overcoming it, so that we may live an abundant life. In Your name, amen.

THE BATTLE BELONGS TO THE LORD PART I

The LORD will fight for you; you need only to be still.
EXODUS 14:14

A few months back, I was sharing with a friend some things I was going through. She reminded me of the story of Jehoshaphat. I went back and read it, and it felt significant.

When I took the Strengths Finder[1] test a couple of years ago, I wasn't surprised to find that my top two strengths are strategic and achiever. When I was homeschooled in 5th grade, I doubled up on my work for 2 weeks so I could take a month off at Christmas. (Go ahead and call me an over-achiever.)

I can be fiercely independent, and I ALWAYS know the best way to do things, get somewhere, and even park. Pray for my husband! He is a laid-back Canadian whose goal is more simplified–he is just looking to get it done, get there, and find a parking spot. Lord bless him. He doesn't even

---

[1] Tom Rath, *Stengths Finder 2.0* (Gallop, Publishing 2007).

seem concerned with the quickest and best ways to do the above. Sometimes it even seems that he doesn't want or need my suggestions. This is shocking, I know. Like I said, pray for the man.

The redeeming factor is my 3rd top strength is connection. That was probably given to me especially for my man. God's grace in this is evident.

One of my biggest passions is that we as the bride of Christ may know Him for who He truly is, and never underestimate how powerful He is within us.

The more I get to know my husband, the more I trust him. The more I watch his character, reactions, humility, and choices, the more I am convicted that my lack of trust in him is foolish. How much more can we trust our perfect Savior than any earthly example of love?

READ 2 CHRONICLES 20:1-30.

What was Jehoshaphat's first response to the news that they were being attacked?

I am amazed by his initial reaction. I know that he didn't have the temptation of an iPhone, but his response was remarkable. The honest truth is sometimes we are far too quick to Google, and too slow to pray. I am convicted of this myself. I want my first reaction to be to kneel down rather than type in a search engine. My solution rests in Someone, not something (information). I have no problem with Spirit-led researching, as long as we get the order right.

Where do you typically run when crisis comes your way?

What are some things you notice about the beginning of Jehoshaphat's prayer in verses 6-7?

I love that he acknowledges that power and might are in God's hands. I also love that he reminds himself of the victories God has already given them.

Your testimonies are powerful! Do you realize that these are times when the God and Creator of the Universe is touching your life?

What does it say in Revelation 12:11?

We overcome by remembering God's faithfulness to us in the past. The enemy is always trying to convince us that God does not have the power or doesn't care enough to do what He has said He will do. When we bring to mind the times when God has delivered us, it strengthens our spirits to recognize that we are once again able to overcome it through Christ! You are more than a conqueror.

What are some times you have seen the Lord deliver you from undesirable circumstances?

What does Jehoshaphat say at the end of 2 Chronicles 20:12?

This is the key! What really matters is what holds our attention. We will continue on with the story of Jehoshaphat in the next lesson.

DECLARATIONS:

I seek the Lord for solutions.

I overcome by the blood of the Lamb and the word of my testimony.

I am more than a conqueror.

I can do all things through Christ who gives me strength.

THE BATTLE BELONGS TO THE LORD PART II

He is the God who avenges me, who subdues nations under me.

PSALM 18:47

Today we are returning to the story of Jehoshaphat, because I am determined to learn how to spell his name… or perhaps, because I think there are still truths that will penetrate our hearts in the latter part of the story.

READ 2 CHRONICLES 20:1-30 AGAIN.

We are jumping right back into the thick of this story. At this point, the people of Judah have just cried out to God for a solution.

What does the Lord tell them to do in verses 15-17?

What did they do when they went out to follow these instructions (verses 21-22)?

After a couple times of reading this passage, I realized something. God didn't tell them to worship.

Praise is a response to who God is, not a strategy. We praise because He is worthy. Period.

I believe that when we lift Him up, He inhabits our praise (Psalm 22:3, KVJ). I believe that when He comes, atmospheres shift. He plays by a different set of rules. He is not inhibited by the same things we are. He is light, and the darkness doesn't have a chance in His midst.

Yet, in all of these things I worship Him because He is worthy, not to get a breakthrough, and that is what the people of Judah did that day. They worshipped because He is worthy to be worshipped, not because that was a part of the strategy!

What happened as they began to sing and praise in verse 22?

How many were left from the other armies?

How many died in Jehoshaphat's army?

What does it say at the end of verse 25?

This is the most amazing part of the story to me! This is the kind of God we serve. Generally, when you enter a battle, you expect losses, but they emerged with NO loss and more loot than they could carry away! This is the kingdom we live in. We serve an awesome and powerful God who is just waiting for you to let Him be God in your life.

I invite you to dream with God about how He can work things together for your good in the areas where you are currently facing resistance.

God not only has plans for you to succeed, He has plans for you to emerge blessed.

What do we know from Romans 8:28?

Ask the Lord what is your responsibility in any current "battles" in your personal life. List them here:

How does the story end in verse 30?

I will take that. Peace on every side... Yes, please!

Are there any areas you feel that the Lord wants to fight for you? If so, how can you turn those areas over to Him?

What are some aspects of God's character that you need in this situation?

Spend time in His presence allowing His Spirit to touch those areas. I am excited for your breakthrough! My prayer is that you too will emerge from this battle with more loot than you can carry.

DECLARATIONS:

He is working all things together for my good.

I am a radical believer in the goodness of God.

I will emerge from this battle with more than I had before the battle.

My God is bigger than any situation I face.

THE BATTLE BELONGS TO THE LORD PART III NEW TESTAMENT

They triumphed over him by the blood of the Lamb and by
the word of their testimony; they did not love their lives
so much as to shrink from death.
REVELATION 12:11

Over the past couple days, we learned about Jehoshaphat and the time that the Lord put three armies "asunder" on behalf of Judah. We read stories in the Old Testament in which the Lord miraculously delivers the Israelites into their promised land. I have good news for us. We have a greater covenant; we are able to step into grace to see victory on even greater levels!

What I am not saying is that if you are facing trials or resistance you are doing something wrong.

What did Jesus say in John 16:33?

We are NOT guaranteed a trouble free existence. Jesus let us know that we will face resistance, but encourages us by reminding us that He has "overcome the world."

What does James 1:2 say about trials of various kinds?

Resistance is what creates muscles. If I go to the gym and do nothing that stretches and challenges my muscles, I won't get any stronger. In the story of Jehoshaphat, we need to realize that they were already in the Promised Land. Their wandering years were behind them, and yet they still faced enemies. The key to their victory was remembering how many times that they had been delivered from various trials in the past, and standing firm in that faith. We are blessed to be New Covenant believers. The blood of Jesus speaks a better word over our various trials (Hebrews 12:24).

What does Isaiah 43:1-2 assure us?

It doesn't say we will never pass through the waters, the rivers, and the fire. It does say that He will be with us, and we will not be swept away or burned.

What does Colossians 1:27 say?

If you are a born-again believer, the One who has overcome the world lives inside of you! I often find we can easily start to focus on what we are or are not doing. We can easily start to condemn ourselves for the hardships we face. My prayer is that today we can brush off those hindrances, and walk in the freedom and grace for which Christ gave His life. Your situation may not shift immediately (although it might), but having the weight of condemnation gone can happen right at this very moment.

READ EPHESIANS 2:6.

The very trials we face today are really underneath our feet! We are seated with Him in heavenly places. The enemy loves to play mind games and try to convince us of our fate, but it is not up to him. We must continually remind ourselves that he has been defeated! Your responsibility is to simply stand firm in who you know God is. That is it. We can relax. We can let go. We can breathe. We can trust.

Does that mean the Lord won't lead you to do anything to overcome this trial? Maybe, but He may also whisper in your ear a way to get out of the pit. His strategies are bathed in peace and hope.

READ COLOSSIANS 2:9-15.

Verse 13 reminds us that Jesus did this while we were dead in our transgressions.

What kind of contribution can a dead person make?

There is not much dead people can offer to their own redemption. The blood of the Lamb redeems us, and we can trust that He can redeem our current battles.

What encouragement does verse 15 bring?

What hope is found in the truth that Christ has disarmed the powers and authorities of this world! The beginning of Colossians 2:14 in the Greek is translated as "paid in full." Jesus already paid for our victory!

Consider the armor of God in Ephesians 6:10-18. Each piece of the armor represents something Christ has already done for us.

Ask the Holy Spirit what He wants to reveal to you about each article of our armor, and how it relates to what Christ has already done. Write it out.

Belt of truth:

Breastplate of righteousness:

Feet fitted with the readiness that comes from the gospel of peace:

Helmet of salvation:

Sword of the Spirit (Word):

What are we to do at the end of verse 13?

This is your responsibility. Stand. Stand firm in the confidence of what Christ has done for you. It's really not about your effort. It is all about the sufficiency of Him. Stop wrestling. Stop fighting. Simply stand.

What is God saying to you through today's lesson?

How can you apply that to any current trials you are facing?

I believe that there is something extremely powerful about believing in the character of God before we see our breakthough that actually releases the breakthrough.

DECLARATIONS:

Like the Israelites and because of what Christ has done, I am well able to overcome this.

His divine power has given me everything I need to succeed.

I can do all things through Christ who gives me strength.

Father, I thank You that because of Your great love You gave Your one and only Son. Teach us today how to walk in the victory that has already been given to us.

LAUGHING AT THE DAYS TO COME

A cheerful heart is good medicine.
PROVERBS 17:22

I love to laugh. A few years back, I went to be a part of a house of prayer team in Washington, D.C. Before I left, I asked my friends and family to pray for abundant joy over me in the new season. I knew that the task at hand could become pretty intense, and that joy would be an important key to longevity. Not far into the year, I was known for my laugh and joy. God was faithful to answer my heart's desire to be filled with His joy.

READ PSALM 126.

What was the fruit of their laughter in verse 2?

Did you know that children laugh on average 400 times a day? Meanwhile the adult averages 30 times a day. No wonder we are taught by Jesus to be like children! People are drawn to children, and I think a lot of that has to do with their joy and ability to let go of things that don't really matter.

My mentor Steve Backlund says to laugh, you have to let go of something. He talks often about when he and his wife are having a disagreement. Often in these moments, we resist any urge to laugh! He jokingly says, "When we disagree, if I laugh that means everything is okay, and everything is not okay."

Have you ever been in a disagreement or argument and suddenly found something so funny that you couldn't resist breaking the tense moment with laughing out loud?

If so, what happened with the disagreement?

Something happens when we laugh. We let go. We stop trying to control. We find rest, and we get a revelation that perhaps everything will be okay.

READ PROVERBS 31:25.

What does your version say?

I love the beginning of this verse. The NIV says, "She is clothed with strength and dignity." What a beautiful picture of the confidence that our heavenly Father desires for us to possess. He doesn't need a people that represent Him walking around staring at the ground. It is a far better witness when we walk this earth knowing who we are and that we carry within us the One who has solutions for every problem (2 Peter 1:3).

I want to focus in on the latter part of Proverbs 31:25.

Here are several versions:

> She smiles at the future... (NASB)
>
> She laughs without fear of the future... (NLT)
>
> She can laugh at the days to come... (NIV)
>
> She shall rejoice in time to come... (NKJV)
>
> And she always faces tomorrow with a smile... (The Message)

Which version speaks to you the most, and what is it that stands out?

Is there anything that hinders you from laughing at the days to come?

How do you think God wants you to feel about your future?

Are there any areas where you don't have hope regarding your future? If so, list them here.

My mentor, Steve Backlund, says, "When I was reading Francis Frangipane's book *The Three Battlegrounds*, I was forever changed when I learned that 'every area of our life that's not glistening with hope means we are believing a lie, and that area of our life is a stronghold of the enemy.' This truth is reinforced by Romans 15:13 and Hebrews 10:23." Look at the areas you listed above, and ask the Lord what is the truth concerning these lies?

God wants you to have a positive emotional reaction to your future. He wants your "heart to throb and swell with joy" (Isaiah 60:5). He is a good Father with good gifts, who withholds no good thing. He takes us from glory to glory.

Proverbs 31:25 is one of my favorite verses. This is God's heart for us. He is a Father who longs to place identity in us that beams with strength and dignity. He longs for us to embrace a hope (confident expectation that good is coming) that brings us to the point of joyous, out loud, laugh-until-your-stomach-hurts laughter when we look to the future.

I pray that today you are "clothed in strength and dignity" and that you can smile, laugh, and rejoice in what tomorrow will bring.

Give any fears you have about your future to Him. He loves you so much. His perfect love casts out all fear (1 John 4:18).

Now to Him who is able to do immeasurably more than all we ask or imagine, according to His power that is at work within us, to Him be glory in the church and in Christ Jesus throughout all generations, for ever and ever! Amen.
EPHESIANS 3:20-21

Now that we've let go of the fears of the unknown, we are free to embrace the mystery and the adventure that our good Father in heaven has for us!

Go ahead… LAUGH, SMILE, AND REJOICE!

DECLARATIONS:

I can laugh at the days to come.

I get excited when I think about my future.

I am moving from glory to glory.

My best days are ahead of me.

CHRISTMAS MORNING HOPE

Little children are God's ongoing witness of His kingdom: a perpetual reminder of what it means to belong to the Father. Children are an unspoken sermon in every home for simplicity, joy, and humility of that which makes the world worth living in. They remind us what it means to be a real Christian.

WINKIE PRATNEY

We love Christmas at our house. Sometime in November, my husband starts asking what I want for Christmas and talking about what he wants.

I love his excitement for Christmas. We both grew up with Christmas being a BIG deal. When I was growing up, we got a real Christmas tree every year. We crammed it into a corner in our living room so that its colorful lights could be seen through the front door by people passing by. It was usually a blue spruce from the state of Michigan (just a slight distance from our Dallas home!) We spent an entire day early in December putting "Christmas" on anything in our house that stood still for long enough. We even had little trees for all of our bedrooms. Good luck finding a room without the Christmas spirit in my childhood home every December!

Christmas morning my siblings and I all waited on the stairs until my mom and dad emerged from their bedroom. It seemed to take forever! I am guessing it was probably about 5:45am. We weren't allowed to turn the corner and let our eyes capture what lay underneath the tree until the family camcorder was rolling. Remember those subtle home video cameras from the late '80s? Dad propped it up on his shoulder and we were finally allowed to turn the corner!

Every year anticipation and excitement flooded my heart. I can't remember a year when I felt anxious about what was under the tree. I knew that my mom and dad loved me, and that they wanted to bless me. I wasn't spoiled, but I knew that my parents loved me and wanted to give me good gifts. I never sat on those stairs sweating and fearing the unknown. Each year we got to give our parents a list of three things that we desired, and I knew I could trust my parents to do what was best for me with that list.

You and I are sitting on those stairs. There are things around the corner that we don't know. There are things in boxes under the tree, and we don't know what is in them. Somewhere along the way we may have lost our ability to embrace the mystery and get excited about the gifts that lie in our future.

What does Matthew 7:11 say?

Are there any "good gifts" you'd like to ask the Father for today? If so, write them out here:

READ MATTHEW 6:25-34.

What is the point of this passage?

What is the best gift you have ever received?

Were you surprised or did you know it was coming?

What made that gift so meaningful to you?

Gifts have the ability to make us feel known. Matthew 7 reveals to us that we have a Father who LOVES to give us good gifts.

Let's sit on the stairs today and pretend it's Christmas morning. I feel that the Holy Spirit wants to wash away past disappointments and to restore our ability to embrace mystery.

Just imagine there is a big Christmas tree behind you, and there are wrapped-up gifts awaiting you. You can let go of the need to know what's in them, and enjoy the excitement and anticipation of receiving!

What can you do today to begin to embrace the mystery of the future that awaits you?

DECLARATIONS:

I am a child of God.

I can confidently expect good things!

I have a good heavenly Father who loves to give good gifts.

NO LONGER SLAVES TO FEAR

You split the sea so I could walk right through it, my fears are drowned in perfect love.
JONATHAN AND MELISSA HELSER

I was in a meeting earlier this week, where the speaker said he thinks that you could trace every problem in the world back to an orphan issue. I was struck by the statement, and began to ponder it. To be honest, I began to ponder the statement in my own life.

How many issues that I face could be resolved if I simply believe in my position as a daughter of God?

I love this scripture in Romans chapter 8, verse 15 (NASB):

For you have not received a spirit of slavery leading to fear again, but you have received a spirit of adoption as sons by which we cry out, Abba! Father!

READ ROMANS 8:14-17.

Who are children of God?

Who bears witness that we are children of God?

How are we able to be sons and daughters of God (see Ephesians 1:5-6)?

It has already been established that if you are a believer in Jesus, and made Him Lord of your life, you are a child of God! The enemy does his best to convince us otherwise.

A pastor friend of ours was telling us about when he recently bought a new car. The salesman was doing his best to convince him that he needed to immediately put down a $500 deposit. This was before he even saw the car! He told the salesman, "Repeat after me–fear doesn't work on Muz." The salesman slowly repeated the phrase, "Fear doesn't work on Muz."

I love this! I think we should put this into practice. What if when finances look impossible we simply utter, "Fear doesn't work on (fill in the blank with your name)?" Relational problems seem unsolvable, so we whisper, "Fear doesn't work on _____." We need a miracle, and so we declare "Fear doesn't work on _____." How much anxiety would this resolve in our daily lives?

Even the secular world agrees that fear has negative effects on our health and our ability to make decisions. I found this excerpt from an article from the University of Minnesota[1]:

"Once the fear pathways are ramped up, the brain short-circuits more rational processing paths and reacts immediately to signals from the amygdala. When in this overactive state, the brain perceives events as negative and remembers them that way.

Living under constant threat weakens our immune system and can cause cardiovascular damage, gastrointestinal problems such as ulcers and irritable bowel syndrome, and decreased fertility.

Fear can impair formation of long-term memories and cause damage to certain parts of the brain, such as the hippocampus. This can make it even more difficult to regulate fear and can leave a person anxious most of the time. To someone in chronic fear, the world looks scary and their memories confirm that.

Moreover, fear can interrupt processes in our brains that allow us to regulate emotions, read non-verbal cues and other information presented to us, reflect before acting, and act ethically. This impacts our thinking and decision-making in negative ways, leaving us susceptible to intense emotions and impulsive reactions. All of these effects can leave us unable to act appropriately.

Other consequences of long-term fear include fatigue, clinical depression, accelerated aging, and even premature death.

So whether threats to our security are real or perceived, they impact our mental and physical wellbeing."

---

[1]Towey, Sue. "Impact of Fear and Anxiety." *Taking Charge of Your Health and Wellbeing*. University of Minnesota. 30 September 2013. Web. 09 October 2014.

Over 150 times in the Bible, we are told "do not fear." I love how God sees things all intricately connected. Science backs up what the Bible instructs us to do! It is actually the best thing for us to follow God's commands. We are told not to fear, because ultimately God is trustworthy. Further still, it is actually good for our physical bodies when we don't give into fear.

He wants us to be so at rest in His goodness that we are able to "laugh at the days to come" (Proverbs 31:25).

We do not have to fear because we are sons and daughters of the best Father we could imagine! He has set us free from the "spirit of slavery which leads to fear" (Romans 8:15). Sometimes it's easy to think that when this (fill in the blank) is resolved, then I will have perfect peace.

Do you remember what Isaiah 26:3 says?

It is the heart of the Father that we walk in peace, not because everything is perfect, but because He is perfect. He has promised even to work the negative things in your life together for your good (Romans 8:28).

READ JOB 42:10-17.

What happened at the end of Job's life?

Job's life was restored to the point that it says, "The Lord blessed the latter part of Job's life more than the first." I believe that the enemy is the one who steals, kills, and destroys, and that when Job said, "the Lord gives and takes away" that was before he had a true revelation of the character of God.

Yes, there is an enemy, but we know One who is greater still. The enemy's favorite tool is fear. He wants us to be enslaved to fear. I believe God is looking for a people who are more impressed with who He is than their current circumstances.

Who He is and who we are in Him can set us free from fear, that is if we are willing to part ways with it. We are His children, and a good Father doesn't want His children to be slaves of fear.

DECLARATIONS:

I am no longer a slave to fear.

He is working all things together for my good.

I trust the Lord at all times.

EXPECTING GOOD THINGS

God is the only one who can make the valley of trouble a
door of hope.
CATHERINE MARSHALL

I grew up in Texas. At my high school, there was one foreign language option and that was Spanish. I didn't mind learning Spanish, but I wasn't thrilled when my guidance counselor put me in Spanish 3 following my request not to be in that class.

A couple weeks after my senior year, I went on a mission trip to Spain that changed my life. In the next few years, I went to Mexico multiple times, Guatemala, Honduras, and Colombia. I was so thankful for the sovereignty of that guidance counselor. I may not be fluent but I can at the very least order a sandwich. I guess Someone really is working all things together for my good.

When I first started to share on the topic of embracing mystery, the Lord reminded me of the Spanish word and definition for hope:

Esperar: to wait, to expect, to hope

Then one day I was reading the Psalms in my study Bible. The Hebrew word *Qavah* is used 46 times in the Old Testament.

Qavah: eagerly waits (1), expect (1), expected (3), hope (3), hoped (1), hopefully wait (1), hoping (1), look (1), look eagerly (1), looked (2), wait (22), waited (7), waited for you eagerly (1), waited patiently (1)

It is the same word used in the following verse:

Wait for the LORD; be strong and let your heart take courage; yes, wait for the LORD.

PSALM 27:14

I find it a little sad that in the English language we separate the words: hope, expect, and wait. "Wait" has become a four-letter word for our Western mindsets, but when it's connected with hoping and expecting, it's a beautiful thing. I believe that God's design is that our awareness of who He is would be so intricately intertwined with our hope that we can't help but expect good things!

What's your reaction to these words?

Hope:

Expect:

Wait:

How are they different?

How are they similar?

How does it change Psalm 27:14 if you substitute in the other verbs?

When I was single and struggling with hopelessness in the romance department, one of my leaders really challenged me in the area of my beliefs. She said to start thinking differently in this area. She said start speaking over my life, "I have options." It reminded me of a sermon I heard where the preacher said, "Orphans don't have options."

When we allow hopelessness to creep into an area of our lives, we are elevating that area over the goodness of our God. We need to be a people who recognize that we have options. We are not powerless pawns on a chessboard.

What does 1 Peter 2:9 say?

Does that sound like we are powerless people?

We are created to be powerful sons and daughters on this earth! I think what's amazing about believing in a great, big God is we realize we have more than one option. We already know what Romans 8:28 says.

It's one thing to expect God to work something out; it's a whole other thing to expect Him to work it out exactly how you see fit. This is really important. Hope does not limit itself to one option.

Embracing mystery is not simply about getting what you want. It's about getting to know the heart of a Father who doesn't withhold any good thing (Psalm 84:11)!

I have fallen into the one-option trap, and it was terrible. I thought that if one relationship didn't work out, I was destined to singleness. Guess what? That relationship didn't work out. It started to turn into something I no longer wanted, and it became clear the same was true for him. I was crushed! I thought I was going to die of a broken heart. I cried every day. I am not immune to a once a month cry, but crying every day was not a good sign. One day God spoke to me and said so clearly, "I am not withholding from you, I am protecting you." God began setting me free and helping me renew my mind to the place of believing I had options.

When my now husband and I discussed the possibility of a relationship, I expressed my interest, and he wanted to pray for TWO WEEKS about if we should or not. The crazy thing is I had tons of peace and confidence through the process. My mind had already decided—I had options. That had become my default. He did not get to define my worth for my Maker already had.

He later asked me how I was so steady and confident during his wavering. I honestly told him, "I trust God enough that if you decide no, He will be faithful to bring someone else in my path." The funny piece is my confidence is one of the things he found himself the most attracted to!

Can you think of some areas where you have limited God to work something out in one way and it didn't work out that way?

If so, take some time to repent for these areas, and ask the Holy Spirit to help you renew your mind for future experiences.

Can you think of any current situations where you need to trust God for more than one solution? If so, what are they?

Today is a new day, and God wants to heal your heart of those past disappointments by revealing to you His love in a greater way. Put on some worship music, and allow yourself to soak in His love. He wants to be big in your life. He wants to turn ashes into beauty. Allow His goodness and presence to saturate your being.

DECLARATIONS:

I have options.

My best days are ahead of me.

There is no situation in my life beyond the redemption of my God.

He satisfies my desires with good things.

DISAPPOINTMENT

We must accept finite disappointment, but we must never lose
infinite hope.
MARTIN LUTHER KING JR

We have all faced disappointment. We hoped for something or someone and it just didn't work out. It's hard to understand and sometimes we need some tools for how to process the pain.

Disappointment is the feeling of dissatisfaction that follows the failure of expectations or hopes to manifest. Similar to regret, it differs in that a person feeling regret focuses primarily on the personal choices that contributed to a poor outcome, while a person feeling disappointment focuses on the outcome itself.

Each time we face a disappointment, we make a choice. Will we be a victim or a victor? I want to share with you some keys I learned at an unlikely moment from King David. This is an excerpt from my blog.

With teary eyes, I sat down with 2 upbeat kids to read them

their bedtime story. Generally I like children, and have a high value for engaging them. This particular evening I was struggling emotionally to get to their 7:30 bedtime so I could have a moment to myself. I was quite relieved when the 3-year-old insisted I play mermaids and sharks with her, only because it required getting into the bed and pulling the covers over my head. The mercy of God can come in such strange ways.

The little boy handed me a comic Bible. I told him to pick one story from the book. He chose 2 Samuel 12. It is the story of David and Bathsheba's first child... every kid's favorite Bible story, right?

As I asked God to hold back my tears for another 10 minutes until I shut their door, He spoke to me through this comic Bible story.

The story begins with Nathan telling David a story. The story is about a rich man who steals a very poor man's sheep. David becomes furious and demands the rich man be punished; the wise Nathan quickly informs David that he is that man. He stole Uriah's wife and killed him. Nathan goes on to tell David that this sin will cost him the life of his first son with Bathsheba. David repents, refuses to eat, and storms the gates of heaven with prayers for his infant son who soon becames sick.

One week later, the child passes away. The servants lurk in the corners of the room, afraid to tell him the news. Let's picture David in the moment. He has not eaten, he has not shaved or showered, and he probably hasn't slept much either. I think I'd be a little afraid, too.

David sees them and he bluntly asks, "Is the child dead?" When they reply that indeed the child has passed, he gets up, eats, takes a shower, goes to the house of the Lord, and he worships.

Let's stop here and read the story in 2 Samuel 12:1-25.

What did David do in verse 16?

Does this surprise you?

How do you think you would have responded to the news?

David believed in God's goodness enough to cry out for the desire of his heart. We need to have so much faith in the goodness of God that we aren't afraid to ask for our hearts' desires.

What does David say in Psalm 34:5?

Does it appear that after David repented in 2 Samuel 12:13 he walked in shame?

I find this fascinating. He repented, but chose not to walk in shame for his sin. The enemy works extra hard to keep us in a place of condemnation. David lived in the old covenant, but walked in new covenant concepts.

Therefore there is no condemnation for those who are in Christ Jesus.
ROMANS 8:1

We will mess up at times, and it's important to repent, take responsibility for our failures, and then let it go. Our focus should be on the Lord, and not on our own shortcomings.

What did David do when his servants told him that the child was dead (2 Samuel 12:20)?

Instead of doubting God's goodness, asking questions, or walking in shame, he worshipped. David knew how to take charge of his soul. He focused his attention on a God worthy of worship rather than focusing on his emotions.

David didn't change his view of God's character when he didn't get what he asked for. We often make the mistake of creating a theology when we don't get what we ask for. We can blame God, others, or ourselves. This is a trap that leads us nowhere.

God is always good. He can redeem any situation. We have the promise of Romans 8:28 that covers the things we don't understand.

When we choose to worship God in the face of disappointment, we exalt Him above the difficulty or problem. In worship, we train our hearts to line up with the truth that nothing is impossible for Him.

Have you ever changed your theology to fit a situation in your life rather than looking to God's word?

READ PSALM 103:1-8.

Who do we discover God is through this passage?

What stands out to you personally?

When we choose to walk in hope, we will probably face disappointment, simply because things don't always happen in our time frame. We can learn from David how to keep our hope on, even when the circumstances around us seem to point to the very opposite.

How did the story with David end in 2 Samuel 12:24?

David went to comfort Bathsheba, and she became pregnant again. They had Solomon, which means "peaceable, perfect, one who recompenses." And we know that Solomon later became the king of Israel.

God took a story full of mistakes, heartache, and disappointment, and brought redemption. He can do the same for you.

I once heard it put this way–"True trust is believing that all His intentions toward you are always good." I challenge you to take hold of the goodness of God and believe that His intentions toward you are ALWAYS good.

DECLARATIONS:

He makes all things beautiful in His time.

The boundary lines fall for me in pleasant places.

I am the head and not the tail.

He takes me to a spacious place.

FISH AND LOAVES

Your hopelessness about a problem is a bigger problem than
the problem.
STEVE BACKLUND

Let's begin with a story I once heard. A young woman told her fiancé, "I flushed my engagement ring down the toilet." He responded with grace and reassured her that he loved her far more than the worth of the ring. The young man passed the test. You see, it was only a test. She didn't really flush it down the toilet! She was testing him to see his true character.

There are many opportunities we face that test our belief in who God is.

READ JOHN 6:1-14.

What was Jesus doing (see verse 6)?

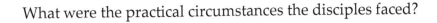
What were the practical circumstances the disciples faced?

When you see lack in your life, what is usually your response?

Personally, I often look to see what I am doing wrong. My natural tendency is to be an achiever. I grew up with a good work ethic. By the time I was in junior high, I had a self-sustaining neighborhood babysitting business going! So when I see circumstances dipping below my comfort sign, I must confess I often look to the wrong place.

Jesus wasn't stressed by the facts. He wasn't uneasy when He was informed about the impossibilities before Him.

I believe that God is inviting us to come into a place where we get excited when we see lack. Don't write me off as crazy just yet! I believe that, like Jesus, we can recognize that our Father is much bigger than any circumstances. We can recognize that every time the enemy serves us lack, it's an opportunity for us to watch the Father show up with His abundance.

Do you ever blame yourself when you see lack in your life?

I am 100% for intimacy with the Lord and allowing the Holy Spirit to convict us when we are off base, but often we can fall into shame and condemnation, which is NOT from Him.

What's the difference between shame and conviction?

Conviction offers hope! Conviction empowers us with the very Spirit of God and a way out! Conviction offers solutions. Conviction doesn't mask itself as shame. Shame puts the focus on us, where it was never meant to be.

What does Psalm 34:5 tell us?

That's it! Our eyes are to be focused and locked on His eyes, not on our circumstances or ourselves.

What did they have in John 6:9?

What did Jesus do first in verse 11?

What are the things you have right now that you can thank the Father for?

Thankfulness is powerful! We enter His gates with thanksgiving, and there are NO limits in His courts. The rules are totally different!

Enter His gates with thanksgiving and His courts with praise; give thanks to Him and praise His name.

PSALM 100:4

What happened in the end of the story (John 6:12-13)?

How crazy is that? They started out with nowhere near enough to feed 5,000 people, and ended up with leftovers! This is our Father.

What are the areas of your life that you feel God wants you to believe for a "fish and loaves" story of your own?

Can you trust Him today with those areas?

Father, I thank You for every fish and loaf we have. I thank You that You are the limitless One. Jesus, I thank You that You came to bring life abundant to us. I thank You in advance Lord for every breakthrough You are going to usher into our lives today.

DECLARATIONS:

My God supplies all my needs.

I serve the God of miracles.

He is working on my behalf.

My true treasures are in heaven.

I am well able to overcome my current trials and test.

OH, TO DREAM AGAIN

A Song of Ascents.
When the LORD brought back the captive ones of Zion,
We were like those who dream.

PSALM 126:1

When I was in the school of ministry, I was challenged to write out a list of 100 dreams. I wrote out dreams and gave myself permission to even list dreams that didn't seem "spiritual." I had dreams that ranged from seeing signs and wonders in Israel to swimming with dolphins, or seeing a whale in the wild.

The next year I went to visit a friend in Hawaii. I was going to be there over my birthday, and she asked what I wanted to do. I mentioned how I'd love to swim with dolphins. I knew that the Hilton there had swimming with dolphins available for a fee.

She started to talk about phases of the moon, and at that point she lost me. I had no idea what she was talking about. Once I arrived in Hawaii, she brought it up again, saying that she thought we could make it work. At this point, I realized she wasn't talking about the Hilton anymore.

We got up early one morning, grabbed americanos at Starbucks, and drove about an hour south. We ended up in what I call "real" Hawaii. There was a large Hawaiian man sitting in a lawn chair with kayaks stacked all around him. We looked into the cove across from him and asked if he had seen any dolphins, and he said they were in the next cove.

We drove a little farther down the road to the other cove. It was a picturesque morning where the sun created beams through the crystal clear water. The cliff was covered in a brilliant green and the water was the most beautiful shade of turquoise. We braved the rocky beach, awkwardly putting on our snorkeling gear, and made our way out into deeper waters.

I pointed out fish as we swam. Suddenly, a mama and baby dolphin swam right underneath me! Before we knew it we were surrounded. A pod of about 50 WILD dolphins was swimming and spinning all around us! We spent about an hour just paddling around, watching them, and listening to them.

I learned something that day that I'll never forget. Our Father loves to fulfill our dreams, and He even loves to outdo what we ask or imagine (Ephesians 3:19-21)!

It was one of the most powerful encounters I have had with God to this day. I felt His love, His care, His presence, and His desire to see His daughter filled with joy and wonder. Having God meet me in that way filled me with hope that He hadn't forgotten the other dreams of my heart. He sees us and He longs to give us good gifts.

What does Psalm 103:5 say?

Do you believe in your heart that He truly wants to "satisfy your desires with good things?"

Is dreaming easy or challenging for you?

Why?

Ask the Holy Spirit if there are any false beliefs that prevent you from dreaming.

One way to cultivate a lifestyle of hope is to compile a list of dreams. Make a goal to list 100 dreams you want to see come true in your lifetime. Take time periodically to look back at your dreams and see what God has fulfilled. Sometimes we can focus on one dream coming true, and lose sight of the other ways God is giving us the desires of our hearts.

The day I swam with dolphins there were still many unfulfilled dreams on my list, yet my heart was so full! I don't always understand His timeline, or why He fulfills some dreams before others, but I do know that being aware of the fulfilled dreams fuels my faith for the dreams I have yet to see come true.

It's so easy to wrap everything up in one dream. I think it's healthy to be children of the King with multiple dreams. My pastor says he never holds God hostage to one thing. I feel that today is a time for you to expand your horizons and dream bigger.

Are you limiting God's goodness to one particular dream or desire?

What are some dreams you have recently seen God fulfill?

Another thing that surprised me about my dream list was how many of my dreams were actually His dreams. He wants to see signs and wonders in Israel even more than I do. He wants to see orphans placed in homes even more than me! The beauty of dreams is that the Maker of heaven and earth weaves His dreams into our hearts.

When we stop dreaming, we do the world a disservice. When we are a new creation, we become one with Him, and we are able to be His change agents on this earth! We get to be a part of making His dreams come true! We get an opportunity to bless the very heart of God by partnering with His heart through dreaming.

I had to overcome the mindset that dreaming is selfish. When I took a step back and read my dreams, I realized my dreams were mostly about others. My dreams were about bringing people into wholeness and an encounter with the God who created them.

So what are you waiting for? Take some time today to thank the Father for every good gift. Then take some time to start expanding your current list of dreams or begin one. From time to time, go back to that list and marvel at what God has done. Have fun, and dream on, my friend. The world is waiting for you!

For the anxious longing of the creation waits eagerly for the revealing of the sons of God. For the creation was subjected to futility, not willingly, but because of Him who subjected it, in hope that the creation itself also will be set free from its slavery to corruption into the freedom of the glory of the children of God. For we know that the whole creation groans and suffers the pains of childbirth together until now. And not only this, but also we ourselves, having the first fruits of the Spirit, even we ourselves groan within ourselves, waiting eagerly for our adoption as sons, the redemption of our body. For in hope we have been saved, but hope that is seen is not hope; for who hopes for what he already sees? But if we hope for what we do not see, with perseverance we wait eagerly for it.

ROMANS 8:19-25

DECLARATIONS:

I love to dream with God.

I love to see His dreams come true through my life.

My dreams come true.

God is faithful and He satisfies my desires with good things.

My dreams make the world a better place.

My dreams bring people into encounters with their Creator!

PROCESS

Life is a journey, not a destination.
RALPH WALDO EMERSON

I had the privilege of spending three weeks in Israel a few years ago. One of the things that stood out to me the most was their understanding of process. In Jewish culture, life is seen as this beautiful, mysterious, unfolding story. Perhaps they are more accustomed to the concept of embracing mystery.

A part of embracing mystery is living life to the fullest in every moment. It's so easy to miss the "God" moments when we rush through life, eyes locked on the end destination. I believe our Father who gives good gifts has them tucked away all along the journey. I believe that He is far too good to only hide gifts at the end destination.

Would you say in this season you are enjoying the process?

READ DEUTERONOMY 6:1-9.

What were God's instructions to the Israelites concerning parenting?

Impress them on your children. Talk about them when you sit at home and when you walk along the road, when you lie down and when you get up.
DEUTERONOMY 6:7

God wants to be a part of our everyday life. For the Israelites He was communicating His desire for them to remember Him as they went about their normal tasks. He wanted them to tell their children of His signs, wonders, and commandments as they went about their daily lives.

In our modern culture I think the end of this scripture would read something like this, "while you are in the minivan, on the airplane, in the grocery store, in line at Starbucks, sitting on the couch, walking to the car from the soccer field." God created life, and He wants to invade every moment. It's not simply about remembering to do what He has commanding, it's about allowing Him to be a part of it all, no matter how mundane or exciting.

I'd like to suggest that God is far more comfortable with process than we are. Think about the fact that He sent Jesus to earth as a baby! He then waited 30 years to begin ministering. 30 YEARS! If production is your goal, then sending a baby is probably not your most logical strategy. I think we are the ones who get frustrated with process, not God. He is so big, wise, peaceful, and capable. He sees time as a servant to accomplishing His purposes in your life.

A few year back I felt the Lord speak this phrase to me, "Waiting speaks of worth." Most good things require waiting. If I want a gourmet steak, it's unlikely I'll find a drive-thru that can fulfill my desire.

We are willing to wait for the things that are really valuable. In this microwave generation, this concept of waiting can be excruciating.

One day I got in a conversation about microwaves with a friend who is undeniably anti-microwave. The things he was telling me were fascinating! He said that studies have shown that microwaving literally changes the molecular structure of a substance.

I am still not anti-microwave. But I do want to challenge our thinking for a minute. Microwaving changes the nutritional value in food, and I think this could quite possibly teach us a great life lesson.

When we skip the process, we may be settling for less than the best that our heavenly Father has for us. Embracing mystery and enjoying the process requires such a deep place of trust. It requires us to wrestle through our fears, in order to find the place of rest. It somehow finds out-of-shape muscles in our heart, and conditions them back to their original design.

What does Isaiah 43:2 suggest?

I think it suggests that we are passing through things. We are moving, and He is promising us His presence on our journey. After all, He is the one who promises to never leave us or forsake us. You are not alone on this journey.

What does John 15:4-5 command us to do?

Connection with the Father is the goal. Connection is what bears fruit. An end destination is not meant to be our goal.

Is there anything that hinders you from enjoying the process?

Often the biggest hindrance to enjoying the process is comparison. When we start to look at the people around us, we can feel behind. Let's think about this for a moment–if God had the same time frame for all of us life would be pretty boring. If we really want to enjoy our own process, we need to embrace it rather than resent it! It's a beautiful journey, and it is yours. No one else gets to enjoy the same journey. Your journey is specifically fashioned for you by the One who knows you best.

The International Standard Version of Matthew 28:19 says, "Therefore, as you go, disciple people in all nations, baptizing them in the name of the Father, and the Son, and the Holy

Spirit." I think that this is God's heart. I pray that as we go, we will spread His love and goodness all around. He wants to encounter us as we are on our way to wherever He is leading us. He is not a Father who only waits at the finish line. He is a Father who runs the race with us.

Go to www.teamhoyt.com and watch the video. I believe this is a beautiful glimpse into our heavenly Father's heart.

He has made everything beautiful in its time.
ECCLESIASTES 3:11

Take some time to surrender to His process today, and enjoy the gifts along the way.

DECLARATIONS:

I embrace the process.

He is making beautiful things on my journey.

I cultivate a thankful heart in all seasons.

I bring people into His goodness as I go.

I trust His process in my life.

My journey is beautiful.

THE GOD OF THE IMPOSSIBLE

Jesus looked at them and said, "With man this is impossible, but with God all things are possible."
MATTHEW 19:26

She slipped through the market, head down, gray wisps slipping past her cloak, with a belly she could no longer hide. In her ninth decade on earth, the Lord saw it fit to open her womb. It had been 90 years, and here she was nine months into the journey of hosting a new life.

It would perhaps have been a greater miracle to leave home and experience the outside world without whispers, giggles, and stares. Yet within her, joy ran much deeper than any shame. She was carrying the miraculous, and the fulfillment of the words of her Maker. In her mind, she couldn't escape watching the smile lines develop on her beloved's face as her belly began to round with each passing month. Sarah knew this was beyond possible with man, but with God, all the facts of this world must submit to One greater.

It wouldn't feel right to write a devotional about hope and leave out our sister in the faith, Sarah. There is so much to learn and glean from Sarah and Abraham's journey of embracing mystery.

READ GENESIS 18:9-19.

What did the Lord tell Abraham in verse 10?

Where was Sarah?

What was her response?

How did the Lord respond to Sarah's laughter in verse 14?

In the following verse, Sarah lied about her laughter to the Lord. His words were too contrary to her circumstances.

Her monthly cycle was long gone. Even in the days when she had a cycle, it seemed to only betray her month after month, simply reminding her that her womb was empty once again.

She forgot the One who spoke these words was the same One who simply spoke this earth we call home into existence. Before we judge Sarah's response, let's examine our hearts.

Are there any areas in your life you have deemed too big for God?

Read Genesis 21:1-8 for the rest of the story.

What does Isaiah 55:11 remind us?

How does that relate to Sarah's story?

What does it mean for you?

I think it's important to note at this point that God fulfilling His word often looks very different than how we think it will look. In the midst of hope and belief for promises, we also need to possess surrender and a trust that allows Him to do it the way He sees best fit.

Embracing mystery is about trusting in His goodness, it is not about locking the Creator of the universe into one possible outcome. It is beyond human logic to open the womb of a 90-year-old woman! Yet, this was the avenue the Father chose to bring His promise to pass.

As the heavens are higher than the earth, so are My ways higher than your ways and My thoughts than your thoughts.
ISAIAH 55:9

Sometimes past disappointments cause us to shut down hope and stop dreaming. This is not the Father's will for us. We are created to be like children, joyfully anticipating the things to come. We cannot divorce hope from faith in His character. His character is more important than our current circumstances. Our circumstances will ultimately bow to His promises. We must learn to look at Him rather than the circumstances that attempt to take our gaze from His face.

Do you feel like you have shut your hope off due to past disappointments?

Now, we are going to journey over to the New Testament version of Sarah. I have good news awaiting you!

READ HEBREWS 11:1-12.

What does it say about Sarah in verse 11? (This passage you may need to look up in the NASB or NKJV.)

Sarah's story was rewritten. In the Old Testament she was the woman who laughed at God! Here she is listed in the famous "hall of faith" as one who "considered Him faithful who had promised" (Hebrews 11:11). She is the only woman mentioned in this passage, and it's quite a raving review.

The good news is that the same can be said for us! Perhaps we have laughed at the promises of God. Perhaps we have considered ourselves too old, too young, too quiet, too loud, too whatever in the past. Perhaps we have limited ourselves. Perhaps we have limited God.

Today is a new day! We can be like Sarah. We can repent (change our thinking), and consider Him faithful who has promised (Hebrews 11:11).

How does 1 Peter 3:6 describe Sarah?

Grace enters the picture and everything changes! Grace rewrites the story. Grace says look at Christ. Grace says He is not limited by your limitations.

I pray that today fresh hope has breathed upon your heart. Nothing is impossible for Him. He loves to use ordinary people to do extraordinary things.

DECLARATIONS:

All things are possible with God.

My God is greater than my circumstance.

I can laugh at the days to come.

I don't give way to fear.

I consider Him faithful who has promised.

HOPE AS AN ANCHOR FOR YOUR SOUL

But blessed is the one who trusts in the Lord, whose
confidence is in Him.
JEREMIAH 17:7

The doctor called one winter night, and it wasn't good news. He called after 5pm, and there were long pauses as he shared the diagnosis. After I hung up, I went and shared the unfortunate news with my husband. The phrase "hope as an anchor for your soul" swept through my mind like a breeze sweeps through trees. I pulled out my Bible, and snuggled up in my favorite chair in search for hope that would anchor my soul and utter a better word over the current diagnosis.

READ HEBREWS 6:9-20.

Which Old Testament hero is this passage referring to?

Can you relate to Abraham (or Sarah)? If so, how?

Are you waiting on a promise? If so, what is that promise?

What do you sense the Father is saying regarding that promise?

Do you have a specific verse that you feel applies to your promise? If so, what is it?

Who did God swear by?

Why did He swear by himself?

People change. Circumstances change. Seasons change. There is only One who is the same yesterday, today, and tomorrow (Hebrews 13:8).

Why might our soul need an anchor?

My soul needs an anchor because the stability this world offers me is not enough. We cannot guarantee much on this side of eternity. But my Jesus, He is a rock. He is a safe, sure bet every time. Certainly not always in the way or timing I thought, but He never leaves me or forsakes me. I need Him to anchor my soul.

One of the definitions of the Greek word for soul is "the seat of the feelings, desires, affections, aversions (our heart, soul, etc.)." An anchor was a common part of their fishing culture, but I think the relevance is even greater than that.

Feelings, desires, affections, and aversions certainly have a way of churning up things and changing within us, much like the sea. Hope, as a result of what Jesus did, is what God gives us to anchor us when the storms come.

We do not what will happen or how it will happen. What we do know is that our God is good. He is working all things together for our good. He wastes nothing. He redeems everything.

Do you need an anchor for your soul today? Take some time and allow Him to penetrate your heart. Allow Him to become more real to you. Let His goodness help settle the ship of your heart into a steady place.

DECLARATIONS:

Hope is the anchor for my soul.

My God does not lie.

God is the same yesterday, today, and tomorrow.

He is working all things together for my good.

He is trustworthy.

114

COURAGE

When God speaks, oftentimes His voice will call for an act of courage on our part.
CHARLES STANLEY

I feel like you can't go far without seeing the word "brave" these days. T-shirts, coffee cups, journals, etc. seem to commonly be decorated with phrases about bravery. It's trendy these days, and I think one of the best ancient biblical examples of bravery would have to be Joshua. Today we are going to go on a journey with Joshua and Caleb.

What did the Lord command him in Joshua 1:1-9?

For Joshua to lead the Israelites into the Promised Land, he would need courage. Oftentimes, we think the receiving of a promise will be the easiest part of the journey. This was a time when they would need to be strong and courageous.

What does courage look like for you in this season?

Keep in mind that courage can look different for each person. For one, courage is to be silent and for another it is to speak up. Try not to compare the areas where you need to find courage to those around you. God is doing a unique process in your heart. It's important to know what that is, and to join in with Him on the journey.

Joshua means savior or deliver. Joshua was a foreshadow of the One to come. He would need courage to defy all human logic to accomplish the things that God created him to do.

What does your name mean?

Do you feel like your name is significant in who you are called to be to the world around you?

If so, how?

If not, who do you feel like God is calling you to be?

My first and middle name mean grace, so my name is "grace grace." For me, courage looks like extending grace. I also lean strongly toward justice. This requires extra bravery for me to let go of right and wrong, and to simply extend grace to those God brings into my life. I have failed many times and sought justice when my responsibility was to extend grace.

Grace: the free and unmerited favor of God, as manifested in the salvation of sinners and the bestowal of blessings

Grace is free and cannot be earned! The Lord gives me opportunities over and over to extend unearned favor and blessings to those precious people He ushers into my life. I share this as an example for you to consider your name, what God is calling you to, and how to apply courage to that.

I believe that God has put you on this earth to express a unique part of who He is to the world. You will need courage to fully express that. Courage requires us to trust in a God who is much bigger than the circumstances we face.

READ NUMBERS 13:25-30.

What did Caleb say in verse 30?

What did the other spies think?

Did they see the same circumstances?

Why do you think Joshua and Caleb's perspective was different than the other spies?

I think Joshua and Caleb took seriously the Lord's command to remember all the ways He delivered the Israelites in the past. The other spies seem to have forgotten the Red Sea parting, the manna from heaven, and the shoes that never wore out.

To have courage for our future promised land, it's important to remember the ways that the Lord has delivered us in the past.

Remember that Ephesians 2 says we are seated in heavenly places. Looking at a situation from a bird's-eye view is a totally different experience than looking up at impending doom. I believe that Joshua and Caleb chose to see the challenge through the lenses of heaven's perspective, rather than through the limits of an earthly view. This is why Caleb could say, "…for we shall surely overcome it" (Numbers 13:30).

Are there any circumstances in your life today that need a perspective shift? If so, what are they?

How do you think those areas look from heaven's perspective?

READ HOSEA 2:14-15.

The word Achor means trouble. The valley of Achor represented a place of pain for the Israelites. God was telling Israel that He would turn their dry (desert) places of pain and trouble into a door of hope. I believe His heart is to do the same for you.

READ PSALM 85:12.

Friend, I believe that God wants to take your places of pain and turn them into something beautiful. He longs to empower you with the courage it will take to step into your promised land. I declare over you that you will surely overcome it.

DECLARATIONS:

I am well able to overcome this.

He is turning the places of pain in my life into doors of hope.

I am growing in courage.

I courageously step into my promise land.

I see my circumstances from heaven's perspective.

THE SIMPLICITY OF ABIDING

May not a single moment of my life be spent outside the light, love and joy of God's presence and not a moment without the entire surrender of myself as a vessel for Him to fill full of His Spirit and His love.

ANDREW MURRAY

I often pray asking Jesus to show me how He lived successfully on this earth. Sometimes the distractions can get so thick that we lose sight of the simplicity the Father had in mind for us.

I've always been a "good" girl. I grew up in church and followed most of the rules. I once got a detention for chewing gum my freshman year in high school, and I cried. If I could go back and tell my 14-year-old self something, I'd probably say, "Relax, you are still going to heaven even though you chewed some gum in biology class."

The terrible part to being a rule follower is that it's easy to get caught up in rules rather than relationship! That is religion, and not what Jesus came to establish on this earth.

Jesus let us in on a little secret in John 5:18. What did he say?

Oftentimes we aren't walking in hope because anxiety is directing our life rather than peace. Anxiety can come from a variety of sources, one of which is that we are taking responsibility for things that are not ours to carry. I believe that walking in peace is crucial to embracing mystery. I think the best way to have peace is to wrap yourself in the Prince of Peace. There is no anxiety in Him. Let Him hold you close until His peace saturates you. His yoke is easy and His burden is light.

What did Jesus tell us in Matthew 11:30?

One of my favorite passages of scripture is John 15.

READ JOHN 15:1-11.

I just love the simplicity of this passage! This is how Jesus lived a life free from entanglements.

THE SIMPLICITY OF ABIDING

What do verses 4-5 say we can do apart from Him?

Wow–that's sobering. In order to abide, we have to let go of our pride. We have to let go of our independence. There is no independence in the trinity. I believe the body of Christ is to look the same.

Hold your place in John 15, but turn to Ephesians 4, and read the first 5 verses.

How many times is the word "one" listed in your Bible in verses 4 and 5?

In the NASB version, it is used 7 times! There is a uniqueness of expression in each of us. There are individual gifts placed upon our lives (Ephesians 4:7). But the goal is for the Body to become a unified expression of who God is.

What does Ecclesiastes 4:9-12 say?

We've probably all heard the expression that there is no "I" in "team." In order to bear fruit, we must learn to abide in the Father. It is more about His presence flowing through us than what we can accomplish in our strength.

Before we go on any further, I am going to ask you to take a moment to ask the Holy Spirit if you need to repent for pride in the form of independence in your life. Jesus said apart from the Father, we can do nothing. It is very important that we lay down our pride, so that we can enjoy the simplicity of abiding in Him.

What does John 15:7 say happens when we abide?

Why did Jesus share these things with us (verse 11)?

How does abiding connect with our hope level in Romans 15:13?

I believe that doing God's will is not about a certain list of tasks or rules. One day doing His will is spending hours in worship and prayer, and another day it may look like taking food to the homeless. It can look like encouraging the exhausted mom at the grocery store.

Doing God's will is about abiding. It's about staying close to Him. It's about fearing Him rather than man. The beautiful thing is that He is fully trustworthy. He is the God of all hope, so we cannot separate Him from hope, love, and peace.

DECLARATIONS:

I am filled with the God of all hope.

I daily abide in Him.

My life bears much fruit, because I abide in Him.

Whatever I ask for is done, because I abide in Him.

His joy is in me that my joy may be full.

I only do what I see the Father doing.

YOUR REAL LIFE

Thanks be to God, there is hope today;
this very hour you can choose Him and serve Him.
D.L. MOODY

As we enter into our last day of this 21-day journey of hope, my heart is full of excitement for you. I am so proud that you have made it through this journey to the end, and pray that your heart has been blessed greatly each time you opened this study.

I pray that you know Him better after completing this study. I pray that your heart has received the peace that passes all understanding. I pray that as you look to the days to come, you are able to smile and even throw your head back and laugh, knowing that your heavenly Father has such good plans for you. I pray that you are learning to truly embrace the mystery that lies before you and the days of fearing the unknown are becoming a distant memory.

For our last lesson, I simply want to cover the simple topic of being present in the moment. We have spent a lot of time looking toward the future and learning to trust the Father. Let's spend a little time focusing on our present season.

What does Psalm 118:24 say about today?

In our culture today, it really requires discipline to be present. For most of us we are just one click away from zoning out of our present reality.

How do you feel like you have been doing lately at being present in your everyday activities?

God wants to meet with you now. He wants to meet you as you pick up your kids from school. He wants to meet you by the washing machine. He wants to meet you in your cubicle at work. Often, it isn't a matter of waiting on Him, it's a matter of inviting Him into your everyday life.

This is your real life. Real life doesn't start when you get the dream job. Real life doesn't start when you finally get married. Real life isn't waiting to happen. Real life is happening whether you engage with it or not. Your real life is now.

What does 1 Peter 1:13 tell us to do?

We are to be fully alert right now! We are to be fully in the season that God has us in, no matter what that may look like. I promise you, no matter what this season looks like, He has good things for you today.

What are you enjoying about your present season?

It's important to be thankful for the good things happening today without dwelling on all the things aren't. My most joyful days are marked more by a thankful heart than by extremely exhilarating circumstances. Sometimes while I am cooking dinner, folding laundry, or vacuuming, I find myself smiling. Is it because those are the most exciting things in my life? No, it is because I can thank and praise God for His goodness in the midst of any tasks!

What does Paul command us to do in Philippians 4:8?

What does Colossians 3:23 tell us?

We can do our everyday, mundane tasks as though we are doing them to the Lord! I used to do laundry for families. Even as I folded someone else's clothes, I could do that unto the Lord.

One day, He began to speak to me and show me all the things He was teaching me through the families I was privileged to be around. I was able to be a part of their everyday lives and see how they made life work in the midst of kids, mission trips, ministry, writing books, etc. It wasn't really about laundry. God opened a door for me to fold their laundry, clean their toilets, and babysit their kids because He was preparing me for my own future.

He is always doing so much more than we realize! If you aren't already, you could be one thought away from enjoying your current season.

What did Paul say in Philippians 4:12?

Do you feel like anything is distracting you from fully being present in your current season? If so, what is it?

Are there any areas where you feel the Lord is asking you to simplify? If so, what are they?

To live with hope for the future doesn't mean you are absent from your current season. Jesus was present in the midst of all His circumstances, and held within Him the vision for how He was going to forever impact eternity.

I pray as we conclude this study that you are learning to balance the tensions. I pray you are able to fully enjoy today while looking forward to what the future holds. I pray that you are experiencing the abundant life today!

DECLARATIONS:

This is the day that the Lord has made; I will rejoice and be glad in it.

My heavenly Father has good gifts for me today.

I am a blessing to everyone I have contact with.

I do small things in a great way.

God is preparing me for great things.

Dear Friend,

I am so proud of you for completing this devotional. I pray that you have a fresh perspective on the unknowns that lie before you. I pray that no matter where it was when you began this journey, you have experienced an increase in your hope level. I pray that like a child on Christmas morning, you are filled with a confident, joyful expectation that good is coming. I pray blessings on you as you continue to embrace the mysteries to come.

With Love,

Anna Maher

For speaking engagements and availability, please visit our website www.chuckandannamaher.com, and send us an email through our contact page. Thanks so much!

Cover Design and Layout Design by Renee Evans Design.
For more information visit:
reneeevansdesign.com

Editing done by Melissa Amato.
For more information please contact Melissa at:
melissa.amato.edits@gmail.com

Made in the USA
Lexington, KY
02 February 2018